A.A.DOYLE

Chihuahuas

Second edition

This book was professionally typeset on Reedsy.
Find out more at reedsy.com

For Daisy,
Forever in our hearts.
We love you and remember you dearly.
There will never be another dog like you. Rest in peace, my angel.

Contents

1

Introduction to the Chihuahua

Haters To The Left

Love them or hate them, the tiny but terrific chihuahua has a way of inciting a strong emotion from either camp. The smallest of all the purebred breeds, this adorable toy breed is very popular in many countries throughout the world, often used in well-known films and TV commercials.

As a faithful chihuahua lover and long-time owner for the past 15 years myself, I have always held a special place in my heart for the breed. Unfortunately, some people enjoy making fun of these miniature dogs, and many times I have been walking my chihuahuas only to be met with sneers from certain individuals passing by, who sometimes call out "What are you walking that rat for?" or "That's not a real dog!"

Chihuahua owners are perhaps just as fiercely loyal to these pint-sized pocket rockets as they are to us. They are intelligent and sassy, very loving and will bond with a particular human in the household quite early on.

They can be very easily trained and do well when competing in agility and obedience trials.

Chihuahuas can also make excellent service dogs, especially for blind people or as emotional support animals.

Some of them even have a special role to play in hospitals working as therapy dogs.

I've never owned a purebred chihuahua, but I can tell you that the chihuahua mixes carry just as much feistiness as their purebred counterparts, and will stand their ground against any foe or intruder who crosses their path.

Here is a little background about my fur children:

Dolly is my first "chi chi" child, and we bonded straight away. I took her to work with me every day in my hair salon, and she responded very well to all of the clients. She spent many days sleeping on the couch in the waiting area, soaking up the sunshine that would pour through the window, and happily receiving pats and scratches from many dog lovers from all walks of life.

My clients were delighted to be in such a sweet little dog's company, and I witnessed the soothing, stress-relieving effects that petting a dog has on humans.

The simple act of petting a dog lowers the stress hormone cortisol and just interacting socially with your dog results in increased levels of the feel-good hormone oxytocin.

This was evident in particular with my father's relationship with Dolly-before he met her, he was not a fan of small dogs in the slightest. He is not an animal person. But before long, Dad was happily taking her for long walks and letting her curl up on his lap for hours. Chihuahuas have a very special way of working their way into their owners (and grandparents) hearts.

Unfortunately, my cat was extremely put-out and no longer felt comfortable being inside the house with us; chihuahuas are often fiercely possessive and protective of their owners, and in some cases, they don't like to share. So be aware of this trait before you invite one into your home.

Once Dolly arrived on the scene, I was no longer a cat person, but a dog person forevermore. When it came time for me to move out of home, my cat stayed with my parents and Dolly was happy to have me all to herself.

A mix of the miniature smooth-coat chihuahua (her father) and silky terrier (her mother), she has a smooth coat and a "deer head". Because she doesn't have the more commonly recognized "apple head", people are often curious about her breed.

With her black and brown markings (now faded to grey and white in her senior years), she has sometimes been compared to a miniature German Shepherd. Her tiny, delicate body fit snugly in the palm of my hand when she was a puppy, but now in her senior years she is quite solid and chunky.

Dolly, now 15, has become the resident salon guard dog. She likes to make herself known to every visitor in the salon with her "ferocious" bark but warms up to many people after a few minutes, and then curls up to sleep for several hours at a time.

Small children and birds have always been her nemeses, however, as she has gotten older they do not seem to bother her quite as much.

She is my best friend and has been my faithful companion from day one. Although tiny, she possesses a big dog attitude and can hold her own in any situation, although I have had to hold her back on countless occasions from getting into hot water with a larger dog when out on a walk, who could easily swallow her whole.

Our scruffy little Betty arrived on the scene when she was 10 years old- Dolly's sister from the same litter. They had not seen each other since a very young age.

I had kept in touch with the breeder's family who had kept Betty as their pet, and one day I received an urgent phone call asking if we could take her in after their American Bulldog attacked her. She was their last remaining chihuahua, as they were now breeding French Bulldogs.

We gladly adopted her, but she had been raised very differently from Dolly and was terrified at first from changing homes and moving to the city from a rural country town. She had never worn a collar or been taken for a walk, so we had to slowly build her confidence with these things.

I was surprised how quickly she did adapt though- initially cowering and running away when I got her collar and lead out, to then leading the charge and jumping in excitement when she realised we were going out for a walk.

I still remember the day she arrived in Adelaide, after a 4-hour car ride. She snarled and snapped at me, but eventually allowed me to gently pick her up and gingerly I took her into our house to be reunited with her sister.

Slowly but surely, Betty warmed to us and became more relaxed. We do have to be careful not to approach her when she is settled on her bed, as we soon figured out this is when she is most defensive and can snarl and snap at us. When she decides to come to you though, she is extremely affectionate and loves to be close to faces.

Even though Dolly sometimes likes the company of her sister, and they quite often snuggle together, I have to say she was happier when she had me all to herself. Now 15 years old, my little old ladies can be grouchy at times and are both going very grey and losing some hearing and sight but are still so loving, can be quite energetic and enjoy their walks. They give me boundless amounts of affection and they crave it from me as well (and from my clients in the hair salon too). They eventually learnt to tolerate my baby twins when they arrived, albeit not too happy about the growing household at first.

Life is constantly enriched by the presence of these beautiful, tiny creatures who can have big attitudes but even bigger hearts.

This Guidebook aims to give you a complete overview and understanding of all things chihuahua, and if you are considering sharing your life with one then I sincerely hope this book can show you just how amazing and loving these sassy little creatures can be. I have included some of my own experiences with my girls as well.

2

Who Are They, and Where Did They Come From?

L et's start with a brief history of our tiny friends. The Chihuahua is the smallest recognized dog breed and is named after the Mexican state of Chihuahua. The breed dates back to the mid-19th century but is thought to be descended from the Techichi of the Toltec people of Mexico as early as the 9th century A.D.

In 1884, the breed was sold by Mexican merchants to border tourists, who then brought them into the US. The dog did not have its official name yet and was often called after the area it had been seen in. It was named the Arizona Dog, the Mexico Dog, the Texas Dog, and the Chihuahua Dog, with the latter becoming the name that stuck.

In the 1890s, the president of Mexico gave a bouquet of flowers to Italian-French opera singer Adelina Patti. Hidden in the bouquet was a tiny chihuahua, and Patti bonded with the dog instantly. She took her new canine companion, named Bonito, across the country for the duration of her tour.

At this time, chihuahuas were talked about but many people had never seen one in the flesh. Patti sparked the beginning of this teeny-tiny dog breed's popularity across the world.

3

It's All in the Details

Apple Head or Deer Head?

A chihuahua's appearance is described as either an "apple head" or a "deer head" in regards to its muzzle and facial structure. Apple head chihuahuas have an apple-shaped head with a 90-degree angle to where the muzzle meets the forehead.

Deer head chihuahuas have a head shape similar to that of a young deer, with a sloped junction of 45 degrees where the muzzle meets the forehead.

It is unknown when or how the breed separated into these two different categories. Both apple and deer heads are depicted in pre-Columbian artifacts from Central America, which suggests that this evolutionary split must have occurred before the New World was discovered by the Europeans.

There are many differences between the two types of chihuahuas- we will begin by taking a look at the apple heads.

Apple heads can have either a smooth or long coat, in any number of colours or combinations of colours.

They have a shorter jawline and a shorter neck than deer heads.

The American Kennel Club only accepts apple-like facial features in its breed standards for chihuahuas.

Due to the shape of their skulls, apple head chihuahuas have larger and more expressive eyes.

They also have short legs in relation to their body length.

Nearly all apple head chihuahuas are born with a molera which is a soft spot in their skull, which usually closes over at 3-4 months old.

Apple heads are the only chihuahuas allowed to compete in the show ring.

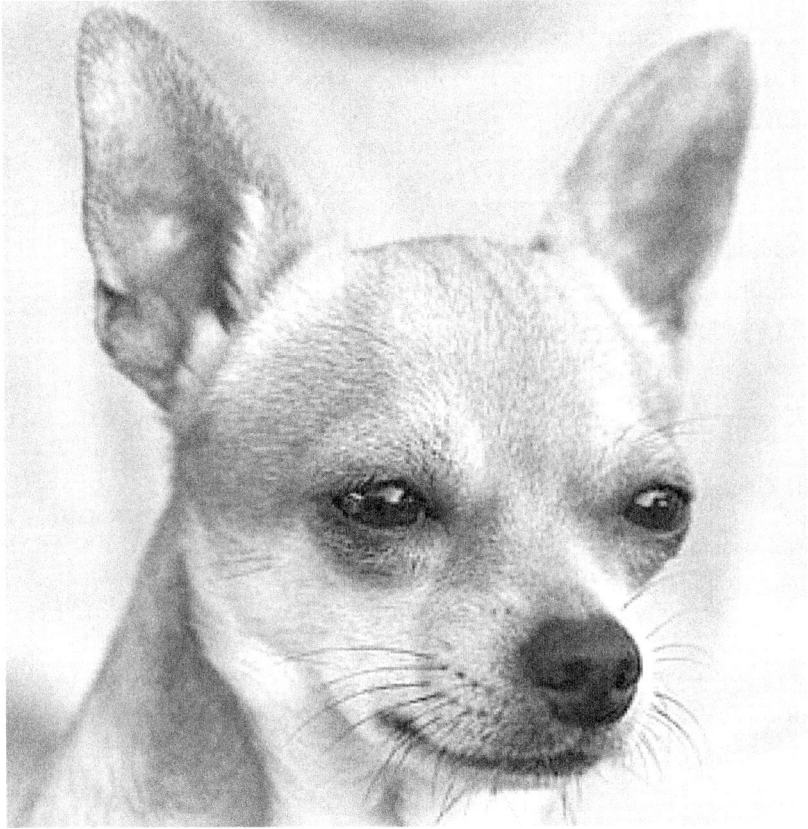

The deer head chihuahua bears a striking resemblance to the facial features of a young deer's face, with a long muzzle, large ears and a sloped forehead.

Deer head chihuahuas can also have both long and short coats, with fawn being the most common colour.

Deer heads are perhaps more popular than apple heads since the Taco Bell dog Gidget was a deer-head chihuahua. Throughout her 8 year career with the national fast food chain, she was responsible for introducing the chihuahua breed to countless Americans.

Many Americans had never seen a chihuahua before. The fact that she was so adorable and fun-loving made the breed skyrocket in popularity during the late 1990s.

Deer heads have a longer muzzle than an apple head, as well as longer legs and taller body height. Deer head chihuahuas have larger ears which also remain erect and upright after being fully developed.
Deer heads have longer necks and jawlines.

Because the AKC refuses to recognize them as an official variety, they are unfortunately disqualified from competing in dog shows.

Moleras do occur in deer head chihuahuas, but the condition is more widely seen in apple heads.

Deer heads are usually larger than apple heads, weighing more than 6 pounds. They are known to be less aggressive and have fewer health problems.

Ears

The ears of a chihuahua are typically large, upright and erect when they are alert. They have a little more of a gap between them when they are relaxed, and when the dog is feeling submissive or fearful, they go down.

Eyes

A chihuahua's eyes are round and dark, and some have a lighter colour than others.

Nose

Typically black or the same colour as their coat in blues, chocolates, reds and blonds. The nose may be pink or tan in blonds or mainly light-coloured chihuahuas.

Height

Male 6-9 inches
  Female 6-9 inches

Coat Colour

Chihuahuas come in over 30 coat colours and combinations. Blue and tan, black and tan, chocolate and tan, white and fawn, red and black, silver and black, white and black, black sabled fawn, black sabled silver, white and blue, blue brindled fawn, blue fawn, white and chocolate, chocolate blue, chocolate brindled fawn, chocolate sabled fawn, cream and white, fawn brindled black, gold, gold and white, red and white, silver and white, silver, white, chocolate, cream, fawn, red, black and blue.

Chihuahuas can be solid, marked, brindled, sabled or splashed.

Tail

Short-coat chihuahuas usually have furry tails, while long hair chi-huahuas have plumed tails with feathering.

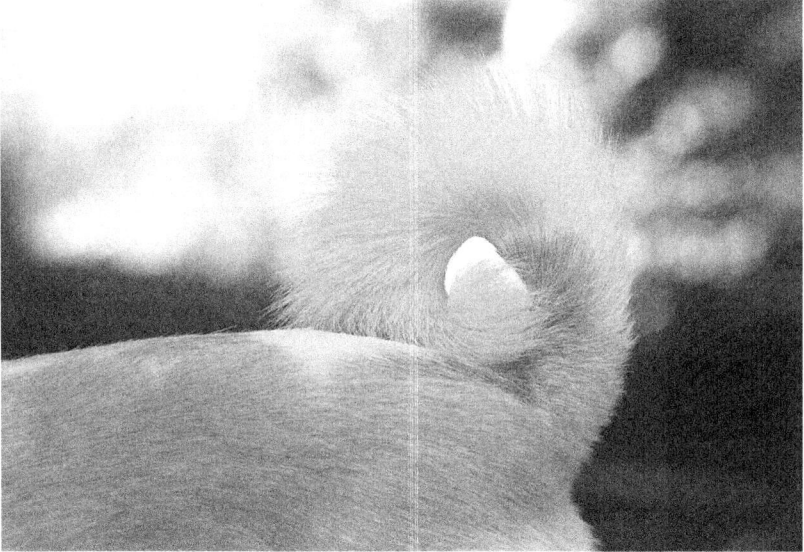

Weight

Male and female chihuahuas average 4-6 pounds. Even though my girls are sisters from the same litter, Dolly has always weighed a lot more than Betty.

4

Here's Something You May Not Know

20 fun chihuahua facts that are sure to blow your mind! How many of these do you find surprising?

1. The chihuahua has one of the longest lifespans, living 15-20 years on average. A key factor contributing to this? The breed has relatively few health issues.
2. The rarest coat colour in chihuahuas is solid white.
3. Two smooth-coat chihuahuas can produce a long-coat puppy due to the long-coat being a recessive gene. However, two long coats cannot create a smooth coat.
4. When compared to all other canine breeds, the chihuahua has the most giant brain in comparison to its body.
5. Chihuahuas make excellent guard dogs, as they have a strong sense of hearing and they are in a constant state of alertness. Although tiny in stature, a chihuahua will bark loudly to scare off intruders and get its owner's attention.
6. A chihuahua named Gidget made the breed famous after starring

in Taco Bell TV commercials. The advertising campaign was worth 500 million dollars, and brought chihuahuas into the spotlight, as many Americans had never seen one before!

7. The word "chihuahua" is one of the world's most frequently misspelled words.

8. Chihuahuas are prone to a medical condition called "reverse sneezing". The chihuahua extends his head and neck while making wheezing noises, as air is pulled through the nose.

9. The Police force in Japan has a search-and-rescue dog named Momo; a 6-pound long-coat chihuahua. Her minute size allows her to crawl through tight spaces and dense rubble in search-and-rescue missions.

10. Chihuahuas typically have "small dog syndrome"- a behavioural condition that describes unwanted actions as a result of the small size of the dog. Chihuahuas will challenge larger dogs when confronted with them by standing their ground and growling, baring their teeth or barking. It is thought that they do this in an effort to compensate for their small size.

11. The largest number of chihuahua pups in a litter is 10, but on average their litter sizes range from 2-5.

12. Chihuahuas are commonly known to shake and shiver, as all dogs do, but this behaviour is seen much more frequently among the chihuahua breed. They do it due to excitability, low body temperature and anxiety.

13. Chihuahuas are categorised as either smooth coats or long coats, with the latter only shedding twice a year and smooth coats shedding year-round.

14. The hair of the long coats is described using specific terms: the tops of the ears are called "Fringe", the leg hair is known as "Furnishings", and the fluff on the tail is called "Plume".

15. When chihuahua pups are born they have floppy ears, which begin

to stand erect as they age. By 6 months their ears stand completely upright.

16. Phobias such as separation anxiety and fear of large crowds or traffic are expected in the chihuahua breed.

17. The smallest dog in the world is a chihuahua called Milly. When born, she was so small that she could fit inside a teaspoon!

18. The Chihuahua Club of America was established in 1923.

19. It was the belief of the Aztecs that the early ancestors of the chihuahua possessed a special power that could take out disease from a human and take on the disease in their own body, as a form of protecting their owners. That myth actually lives on today!

20. The most popular chihuahua names have remained the same for quite a few years, with the top name being Bella. Other popular names include Coco, Lola, Daisy, Peanut, Luna, Chloe, Lucy, Max, Charlie and Buddy.

5

You Can Tell It's a Chihuahua When…

Chihuahuas are widely known as tiny dogs with larger-than-life personalities. They may be one of the most misunderstood breeds in the world and can be complicated little creatures.

Negative first impressions can scare away some prospective owners, but hopefully, most people can ultimately see the funny side of the slightly aggressive temperament that the lovable chihuahua can portray. They truly are big dogs in little dog bodies.

There are many wonderful aspects and advantages to owning one of these tiny canines (or rather, a chihuahua owning its human), the first of which is their size which makes them extremely portable and convenient.

You can easily carry a chihuahua, whether it's in your pocket or in a baby carrier.

When Dolly was a little pup, I carried her in a dog carrier handbag to work and to the shops. She would eagerly dive in head first the very second that she saw me grab my keys. There was no way she was going to miss out on an outing with Mum.

As they are so small, they only require half a cup of dog food per day, which makes them very economical. How's that for a budget-friendly dog?

The chihuahua's temperament also makes them wonderful guard dogs. Their fully erect ears help them to be able to hear strangers and other dogs long before they come into view.

They have very few health problems, so this means fewer vet bills. I have found this to be very true over the last 15 years, even in recent years now with the two dogs.

As chihuahuas are so little, you do need to pay careful attention so as not to injure them or accidentally step on them. They have a delicate bone structure and can easily be overlooked when they are underfoot.

My Dolly has always been very nimble and agile- in her younger years, she could quickly gauge where people were about to step and scurry out of the way.

One aspect of their temperament that is a little more undesirable to some is the fact they are not good with small children. Under the age of six, energetic children who get too close will generally get bitten or growled at.

Children typically want to pick chihuahuas up because they are little and cute and look like toys, not realising how vicious they can be when they feel threatened.

Chihuahuas can get grumpy even when children aren't touching them but are just in their vicinity, and their comfort zone needs to be respected.

Although not always true for each dog, chihuahuas typically only like one person, and may not accept your friends and family. Great care should be observed when taking your chihuahua out to public places such as the dog park.

Your chihuahua is happiest when with you and you alone!
Even if you socialise them from a young age, they will be most comfortable around you and depend only on you.

My partner always found it funny when I was working late, and he would give Dolly her food. She would totally ignore her dinner until I walked through the door.

Overall, their loyalty and loving nature far outweigh any negative traits. Chihuahuas make wonderful lifelong companions, all they ask for in return is food and a nice warm lap.

6

Training Time

Chihuahuas are very intelligent, but can also be strong-minded and stubborn. This can sometimes make them difficult to train, but not impossible.

Reward-based methods can be appealing when training your chihuahua to be obedient.

Training should begin from an early age so they don't grow up to be aggressive.

The chihuahuas' attachment to their owners can lead to dominant behaviours and they need to be socialized with other dogs and people in order to avoid potential aggressive behaviours in the future, such as:

-Displaying little dog syndrome
   -Being suspicious of other people aside from their owner
   -Growling/biting small children
   -Overreacting to noises from outside

Chihuahuas can believe that they rule the household if given the chance.

You must take control of the household before they do!

Below are some of the most important basics when training your chihuahua:

Establish your boundaries and take your position as top dog.

Feed your chihuahua at set times every day. Do not let the dog decide when it wants to eat. This will show the dog who makes the decisions in the house, and it needs to get in line and obey.

Chihuahuas can be walked twice or more in a day, but always make sure that you control the walk. Never let the dog pull you in a different direction- leash control is essential when training a chihuahua.

Set restrictions and limitations on what furnishings the dog is allowed to jump up on, and which ones he isn't. Don't respond to barking or whining.

Don't give the dog attention when he is over-excited as you enter the house. Instead, only pay him attention when he has calmed down.

Many chihuahuas do not get enough emotional stimulation or exercise. Always make sure to take the dog to parks to play fetch etc. Use basic commands to coach such as sit, stay, speak, and quiet.

The best way to educate a chihuahua is by diminishing the opportunities for the dog to challenge you, or to be overcome with boredom and unused energy. This will ensure that the negative behaviours widely looked down on will not eventuate.

Training a chihuahua takes a great deal of patience, commitment and creativity. The trainer must be well-versed in the chihuahua's temperament to have any success in teaching the dog to perform tricks and obey basic commands.

Since chihuahuas are energetic, intelligent and very lively, they enjoy physical activities and doing things that stimulate their brain.

Training involves both of these components, so chihuahuas do respond well when the training is carried out correctly. Plenty of encouragement is also needed, as well as rewards and constant praise. These are all crucial elements in your chihuahua's training.

What to Teach Your Chihuahua

Patience is vital when training a chihuahua. You should avoid training when you are not in a good mood or tired. Take your time and always prepare your treats before you begin a lesson. It is also important to toilet-train the dog at an early age.

Basic commands include:

-Sit
  -Down
  -Stay
  -Come
  -Heel
  -Roll over

A helpful tip is to put your chihuahua up on a table while you are teaching these commands, so you can avoid bending down all the time.

Crate training should help your dog to know the right place to do their business in the house. Bring the puppy to the crate after eating, as soon as he wakes up or when you see him circling. Puppy pads can also be used.

Handling Your Chihuahua

More than anything else, you need to be gentle with chihuahuas. Never use choke collars on a chihuahua as their little necks can easily be injured. Instead, use a flat buckle collar or harness to avoid any damage to their trachea.

Exercise should be a top priority and should be offered every day where possible. Chihuahuas do not always need long walks as they naturally burn off plenty of energy due to their energetic nature. Another bonus!

Take special care when taking your dog out in cold weather and dress him in a warm coat as toy breeds are very sensitive to cold temperatures. When the temperature is extremely cold, they should not be taken outside. They much prefer to stay snuggled up on the couch in a soft, warm blanket.

Be careful if your pup decides he wants to jump down from your lap or a sofa. A chihuahua should never be allowed to jump from a high place to avoid hurting its joints due to the impact when landing.

7

Which Foods Will Keep Your Chihuahua Healthy and Happy?

Careful thought must be taken when deciding what to feed your chihuahua. These dogs can be very sensitive in regard to what kind of food they are being fed, the feeding schedule, and how the food is presented to them.

Your puppy or dog's health now and in the future will depend greatly upon what you feed them, so it's important to do some research.

Chihuahuas cannot tolerate too many chemicals from artificial colouring and preservatives. They need a good balance of healthy fats, protein, and healthy carbs. Sometimes you will need to experiment to find out what type of ingredients your chihuahua prefers and can tolerate with his sensitive digestive system.

If your chihuahua is not thriving on his current diet or if you notice an intolerance or allergy you may need to change his diet. It is best to do this gradually.

Toy breeds such as the chihuahua can be fed small, frequent meals depending on their age.

For puppies 3 months and under, free-feeding is recommended. Leave food out where they can access it at all times, day and night. Make sure to refresh it before it becomes old and stale.

Most chihuahua puppies from 3 months on and chihuahua adults do well with 3 meals per day, as well as snacks in between.

Treat dispensing toys are a great option as they can be filled with a meal's worth of food and will keep the dog busy, especially if you are not at home during the day to spend time with it. Just make sure you can find a food dispenser toy that is small enough for your chihuahua's tiny jaws!

How you time the evening meal will affect the dog's morning bowel movement, so keep this in mind and adjust if need be.

Chihuahua puppies require approx 50 calories per day, and adults need 35- 40 calories for each pound of body weight. A chihuahua that weighs 4 - 10 pounds will need to eat generally ½ to 1 and ⅓ cups of food per day which is split into 3 meals throughout the day.

This is obviously a much smaller portion of food than the amount that is required for larger dog breeds which is another fantastic advantage of owning a small dog.

Good quality food is needed for optimal energy levels and to build muscle, and will play a big role in determining the outcomes for the dog's short-term and long-term health.

A dog's diet correlates closely to skin and coat health, organ and immune system health, as well as some diseases and cancers.

Some behavioural issues such as hyperactivity have been linked to certain ingredients found in dog food, so this is something to be aware of also.

A wide range of issues can evolve from an allergy or intolerance to certain ingredients, including hives, rashes, itching, digestive issues and hot spots.

You can tell if a chihuahua is being fed properly as he will have a shiny coat, no skin problems, bright eyes, good energy levels and overall good health.

When looking for the best food to give your chihuahua, keep an eye out for the following elements:

100% natural- this means no artificial colouring, flavours or preservatives.

Wholesome protein from traditional meat or fish, with the meat being whole or meal.

Avoid cheap fillers such as corn and cereal grains.

Glucosamine and chondroitin for healthy joints, probiotics to aid with digestion, antioxidants for a good immune system, and sufficient levels of omega fatty acids for optimal skin and coat.

Correct ratios of protein, carbs, fat and fibre.

Home-Cooking Chihuahua Food

If your dog has an intolerance to manufactured food or is very fussy, it might be best to make their meals from scratch at home. Make sure to include a wide range of healthy ingredients to make up a well-balanced diet for your chihuahua. Weekly meal preps will help you to manage the time you have to spend in the kitchen.

Wet Food or Dry Food?

Most dogs seem to greatly prefer wet food over dry, however, hard dry kibble is important in keeping their teeth and gums healthy and clear of disease. A mixture of both wet and dry foods will assist in healthy bowel movements as well.

If your chihuahua refuses to eat the dry food, you can try drizzling it with a broth or warm water to soften it up and make it more appealing.

Toxic Foods to Avoid:

Shallots
  Onion
  Garlic
  Chives
  Leeks
  Grapes and grape flavours
  Chocolate
  Currants and currant flavours
  Raisins
  Wild mushrooms
  Pecans
  Walnuts
  Macadamia nuts
  Cherries

Fruit pits and cores

Apple seeds

Foods containing xylitol

Caffeine

Leaves and other parts of tomato plants, avocado plants, bell pepper plants and eggplant plants.

Yeast dough

Note: Milk can cause loose bowels and an upset stomach but is not toxic.

Fussy Eaters

Chihuahua owners will often worry that their dog is not eating enough or is not happy with his food. More often than not, this is more just a case of chihuahuas needing less food than the owner realises. Some dogs appear fussy or finicky about their food, but rather they are just eating only what they need.

As long as your chihuahua puppy has a steady weight gain or your adult chihuahua is maintaining its weight and being fed high-quality food, there is no need to worry. He is simply eating what he requires.

An abrupt change in diet can signal a possible health issue- if your chihuahua loses weight then a visit to the vet will be required.

8

Groomed and Gorgeous

B oth short-haired and long-haired chihuahuas need regular bathing and brushing.

Brushing once a week is enough for short hair, and long-haired dogs require brushing 3 times a week where possible. Brushing and trimming on long-hair chihuahuas is most important, in particular on the legs and tail. This will help the fur to avoid getting matted.

Don't clip or shave your chihuahua's fur in warm weather, as the fur protects them from the heat. If their fur is too short, it can lead to sunburns and heatstroke. A bath once a month is sufficient unless they have been rolling in the mud. When bathing your chihuahua, don't use shampoo on its face. You want to avoid getting shampoo in its big eyes and causing irritation. A damp washcloth can be used to wash the face instead.

The short-haired chihuahua is one of the simplest dog breeds to maintain in regard to grooming- another great advantage.

You will however need to learn how to safely handle him with confidence so you can avoid your chihuahua getting nervous and stressed out while being groomed.

Rubber curry brushes help with de-shedding while massaging the dog in the direction of hair growth. They can be used during bathing for a cleansing massage too.

If your chihuahua has pockets of built-up shed hair called "packing", you will need a wire slicker to remove them. Take care to use a gentle slicker to protect their sensitive skin.

If strong odour is an issue, make sure your dog's diet contains omega-3 and omega-6 fatty acids and antioxidants for a beautiful coat and healthy skin.

Nail care can be tricky, so have someone assisting you to gently keep your dog from squirming around too much, but never apply too much pressure on the fragile neck or throat.

Start with the back paws and nip the tips to begin with, all the while offering praise to keep your dog calm. Repeat for the front nails, and avoid squeezing or twisting the legs.

In the case that you nick the "quick" (the vein inside the nail), have some styptic powder close by to quickly dab on the affected nail.

A pet's walking ability can be impacted by overgrown nails, and in severe cases even deform the dog's feet if left untrimmed for too long.

Dental disease is commonly seen in chihuahuas, so regular dental care is a must. To reduce the chances of dental disease occurring, brush your dog's teeth once a day and have your vet do a professional dental clean once yearly.

I found that Dolly greatly despised me trying to brush her teeth, and over the years she did have to have some teeth removed. Now she has no teeth left, and her tongue frequently falls out of her mouth, which you do see quite a bit in senior chihuahuas.

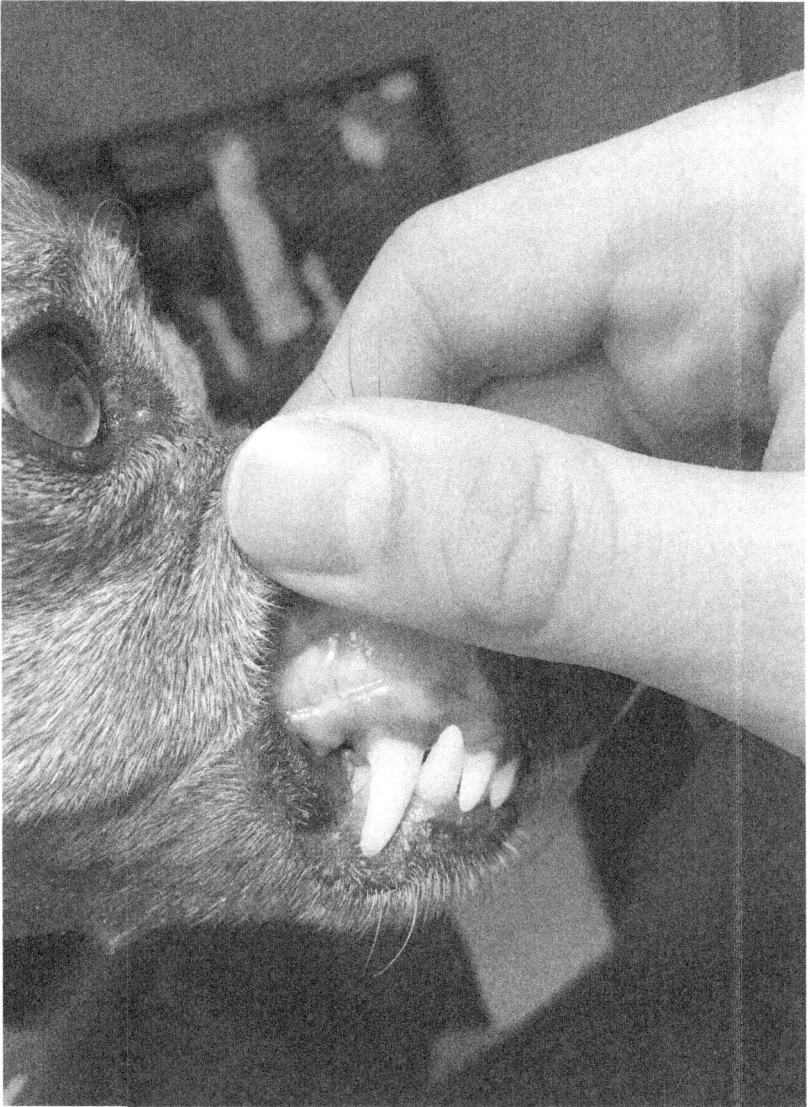

Help the dog to become familiar with the sensation of brushing their teeth while they are young pups so that they don't resist it when they are older. A dog groomer or a vet can assist you with doing this correctly.

Pay close attention to your chihuahua's eyes while grooming - as they have large, round eyes they can be prone to eye issues. This can happen more often in older dogs. Examples of these issues include dry eye, cherry eye and glaucoma.

We have certainly seen this to be true in Betty's eyes, as she has had a couple of eye surgeries now, and does suffer from dry eye and glaucoma, both luckily controlled with daily eye drops.

Conclusion: Is A Chihuahua Right For You?

The chihuahua is a tiny dog that possesses big dog energy and has a whole lot of love to give. They are ideal for singles, retirees and apartment living. Challenges may arise for those who have young children, other pets, or have a job that demands much of your time away from home, as these loving balls of energy want to be around you as much as possible.

I hope that the information provided in this book can help you to decide whether the chihuahua is the right breed for you and if the answer is yes- you are in for some wonderful adventures and endless snuggles with your ever-loyal new best friend.

If this book proved helpful for you, I would greatly appreciate it if you could take the time to leave me a positive review on Amazon so that this book can reach more people who want to know more about the amazing Chihuahua breed.

If you are a fellow chihuahua owner, please leave a review about your own experiences raising your dog/s. They are a special type of animal who just want to be loved, so let's clear up the misconceptions surrounding their breed. Thank you for reading.

RESOURCES

Chihuahua Breed of Dog Britannica. (n.d.). Britannica. Retrieved June 28, 2022, from https://www.britannica.com/animal/Chihua hua-dog

History of the Chihuahua Breed. (n.d.). Chihuahua Wardrobe. Retrieved June 28, 2022, from https://www.chihuahuawardro be.com/history-of-the-chihuahua-breed/

60 Amazing Chihuahua Facts. (n.d.). Chihuahua Wardrobe. Re-trieved June 28, 2022, from https://www.chihuahuawardrobe.co m/60-amazing-facts-about-chihuahuas/

12 Fun Chihuahua Facts You May Not Know. (2018, March 5). Central California SPCA Fresno's Humane Society Since 1895. Retrieved June 28, 2022, from https://www.ccspca.com/blog-spca/educatio n/chihuahua-facts/

10 Facts About Chihuahuas. (2022, April 1). Mental Floss. Retrieved June 28, 2022, from https://www.mentalfloss.com/article/64317/ 10-feisty-facts-about-chihuahuas

Chihuahua Temperament: The Good, The Bad and The Ugly. (2022, April 21). Pet Helpful. Retrieved June 28, 2022, from https://pethe lpful.com/dogs/A-Chihuahua-Temperament-The-Good-The-Ba d-and-The-Ugly

Feeding Your Chihuahua- Amounts, Timing, Best Food. (n.d.). Pet Chi Dog. Retrieved June 28, 2022, from http://www.petchidog.com/chihuahua-food-feeding

Grooming a Short Hair Chihuahua. (2021, April 20). Bechewy. Retrieved June 28, 2022, from https://be.chewy.com/grooming-a-shorthaired-chihuahua/#:~:text=When%20it%20comes%20to%20grooming,powder%20to%20do%20the%20job

Deer Head vs Apple Head Chihuahua: What's the Difference? (2022). Chihuahua Wardrobe. Retrieved June 28, 2022, from https://www.chihuahuawardrobe.com/deer-head-vs-apple-head-chihuahua-whats-the-difference/

Printed in Great Britain
by Amazon